OBSERVATIONS AND COMMENTARY—ONE HUNDRED POEMS

OBSERVATIONS AND COMMENTARY
—
ONE HUNDRED POEMS

by
Tom Spence

Sastrugi Press
Jackson, WY

For permission requests, write to the publisher, addressed Attention: Permissions Coordinator
Sastrugi Press, P.O. Box 1297, Jackson, WY 83001, United States.

www.sastrugipress.com

Library of Congress Catalog-in-Publication Data Available
Spence, Tom
Observations and Commentary / Tom Spence- 1st United States edition
p. cm.
1. Poetry 2. Philosophy 3. Nature

Summary: A volume of poetry.

ISBN-13: 978-1-64922-223-7 (hardback)

Sastrugi Press
00243

Printed in the United States of America when purchased in the United States

10 9 8 7 6 5 4 3 2 1

~ FOREWORD ~

Tom Spence is an extraordinarily gifted writer. His poetry can approach an e. e. cummings sense of play on the page, with a profound honesty and depth of feeling.

Fathoming our paths in the large and small schemes of life, with puns and arrows to guide us, is a humble voice (the word "i" is always lower-case), captivating readers.

"love   has many expressions   that s why i didn t eat a single one of her mother s day chocolates while she was off visiting her grandchildren"

And, with relatively little punctuation, except for an occasional forewarning that a question or exclamation is coming, Tom's poems are formatted to show the reader the pace and pulse at which he wants them read.

"(?)but can you hold that thought   i m trying to concentrate & you have interrupted me   you know   at my age learning something new isn t easy"

His themes, often universal and personal at once, can spark many a reflection or smile:

"an itch   demonstrates a   perfectly coordinated world   i arrive in the   garden simultaneously   with the   fly   that bites me"

Tom writes every day, and his immediacy is refreshing. Even though his first poem describes his work as "daily   verse   not for (accidental) art   but for practice," in truth Tom is the only person I know who grasps the significance of, wrestles with, and/or accepts what each day brings – and straightaway turns it into art.

Spoiler alert: A few words (mulligrubs, traducer, casuistry) might drive you to the dictionary. But these are few and far between – and it's worth the education.

I have enjoyed Tom's work for several years, and I'm thrilled that he now has a book to share with the world!

— Carol L. Deering, author of HAVOC & SOLACE: POEMS OF THE INLAND WEST.

Each poem which follows...

...has a date below it because that signifies the day (more or less) of its inception.

However, the order in which the poems are presented is different because adjacent poems might in some way be commentary on each other. Often a poem just found a comfortable place to settle.

Explaining the origins, inspirations, or purposes of a collection of poems can get boring and is usually pointless. So, I've refrained from it.

As far as the production of this volume, I've had excellent help, and I've needed it:

- Interpreting the signals—some a nod and smile, some with arched eyebrow or sigh—from Vikki Chenette, my mate; and her loving me, tolerating me between times, is mostly what got me here.
- I wish my insights were half as sharp as those of the eyes of my friend, Carol Deering, who helped with the editing. Great thanks to her!
- Aaron Linsdau at Sastrugi Press is capable and patient beyond reason. So, the volume is done right.
- Other readers and "blurbers" made me think a little better of myself. Thank all of you for that.

Tom Spence

daily

verse   not for (accidental) art   but for practice   so that
(if the moment comes) a timely launch at that critical moment
when (pretending that)   everything depends on the moment
the release will be subtly automatic   the trajectory accurate   toward
→ the chosen target   discovered for a moment out
from shelter & which if missed   at least will be (folded into
future tents   & startled away   from smug momentary invulnera-
bility) in a manner of speaking

5.15.20

pill bottle

spilled (oops)
no (doubt) an offering from
the muse s clumsy hand
(ah poesy)

pills not
exotic   (n)or toxically suicidal
anodynes for dread   or
despair

nope   just little capsules
for calming acid reflux
and other
aesthetic insights

5.14.20

intrepidity

you are co evolved with foolishness   a verse of affection
blushes disrobed   name describe & implicate   expose
wh (*at* or *om*) you love
                    avow →it← publicly   for love abases
enervates   displaces   selfrespect&freedom   but it
hurts like fun   (!) b-brave fool   it s too late
for circumspection

5.16.20

cold

february morning   sub-zero warns me   that disaster s imminent
unless i m wrong   something s on the way that s going to go
badly   a prejudice unproven   &   after all desperate people have
thirsted in the heat   & comfortable people have collapsed to
infarctions   (mid sentence in mid june)   & naïve
people of hope & in good faith   & good spirits have been felled by
random irony, metastases, careless driving   grand strategies   &
good intentions   with bad outcomes   that s what s so
charming about speculating   about what disasters are chilled
lying about   waiting   & probably just about to happen   to
the forsaken   in the february cold

2.6.21

once

a friend who worked in the   e r   told me that a graffiti
                              in the restroom [stall] said
        SOMEWHERE   SOMETHING'S GOING WRONG
at the time it sounded optimistic   like
job security or as if
failure wouldn t discourage the resolute
      now it sounds like
                              resignation   like
                              nothing can be done
                              or   should be done
                              even if it could be done
                      as if anyone were willing to try
                              or was way past done
                                            trying

2.12.21

love

has many expressions   that s why i didn t eat a single one of her
mother s day chocolates while she was off visiting her grandchildren

love s power is entangled   with paralyzing fear & supported by
inexplicable self discipline

5.24.21

learning

i ve discovered   doesn t always come before knowing   &   i don t
know how many things i ve learned   (& please   don t ask)   but
i know you love me   because you ve told me so   & you ve shown
me so   (& so)   while knowing i am loved   i promise to learn
how to love you better (as practicing makes imperfect)   but   oh
how disappointed i will be   if i proclaim   i love you   more
& more   & better & better   than i did before

                                              &   you answer
(!) i knew it all along

                    (?)but can you hold that thought   i m
trying to concentrate & you have interrupted me   you know   at
my age   learning something new isn t easy

3.17.21

when

my application is processed   & i m finally put in negligent charge of
things great & small   events
              & venues   surprises
          & sacrifices   (did I say?) plans
                                        i plan to announce my
dereliction & abdication from planning   matters will be settled by
settling   things moving at the very first tick will be on their   own
(out of my hands)   i plan to contemplate cause   & effect & other
common things about which nothing is known   & i plan to watch my
crumpled check list   freed from the refrigerator door   bouncing
ahead of the wind

5.18.20

a quick catalogue

of what I know: to be honest about it   i am comfortable with the
gnawing sound from the termites of doubt   the utility of relativism
is that i didn t mean what i meant   when i suggested that i might
know something   & i ve been meaning to confess that   (if you
know what i mean....)

4. 1. 21

i ve abandoned

my expectations   i should know better   & i shouldn t expect so
much   flirting in the afternoon   catching your eye at the end of
the day   listening to the radio in the twilight & imagining how it
might be to imagine i know how it might have been   the feint of a
couple of hopeful days   then slipping backward   ah spring   you
remind me of my yearning fickle youth   inconstant   & which
surely i haven t invented to replace what i ve forgotten   which is all
wrapped up in vaporous waking dreams   fanciful & frivolous

4.6.21

blundering

offers opportunities which a
     plan would eliminate

what s important   isn t
urgent   what s urgent isn t
on the way   what arrives
is unexpected   imagine

the   1st glimmer of
consciousness   & the
response   that s not what
i had in mind   at all

5.27.20

t ain t

funny
mcgee   but only someone who thinks too much   will think he
shouldn t laugh at the nonsense   it s the best way to
express the trouble we re in   &
the best joke aims at the   victim
who most enjoys it

12.9.20

(?)what

was the shape of
that recollection   you know   the
fragrant one   the sun on the water
& time endless

6.28.20

morning

a stunning arrival   not the one i requested   a triumph
nevertheless   both of timing & delivery   not belying
the catalogue s overwrought pitch
                                        of sunrise   promise
striated sky   & singing wind   (all)
supporting my hopeful plans   & here i pause to consider
                                        my part in the bargain

2.1.21

stop me

if i borrowed this theme   even if you don t remember   &
i ve forgotten it   i m sure i must have asked   so   stop me
if i asked and then forgot   what the theme of this poem was
though you must have had an idea   but didn t remember that
you forgot   &whose job it was to write it down (→?)

5.30.20

my anger

has muscle memory   it bursts the doors of the closet for the
appropriate costume   the once naked creature now attired for
the occasion   an aggrieved jester   informed soon after leaving
his dressing room that he is not only foolish again   & clownish
but no clown

5.5.21

late

i ll put it away until morning when the big
eye
winks orange on the horizon   to inform
me that what s trite   comes in many
other colors of deception   & repetition

1.3.21

accusing

eyes of day
almost audibly the silent clock ticks the minutes

(?) am i late in completing something for which assignments i wait as
if they hadn t been delivered on the winds of consciousness

                                                                    noises
repeated for breath   wasted   by disguising deception as deliverance
& wasted more on excuses than excesses   & wasted still by
substituting regression for remission & regret

1.31.21

rehearsal

preparing for life   it s a new act every day   i ve learned my
lines   practiced them so they seem almost natural   almost
spontaneous   my temporary positions on the stage are marked
i own my space as if i belong there

                                    & when the cue line arrives   if it
arrives   i m distracted by living   & miss the moment   & its
fine monologue   &...   its heroic gesture

4.17.21

everybody

(even those who don t know) knows e e cummings line   (" ")
colossal hoax of clocks and calendars

compounding that hoax is sunrise   8 hour workdays   overtime paid
& unpaid   who s early & who s late   a pushpin   or   postit
denoting whose birthday slipt by unnoticed & uncelebrated   (worthy
of a shun or a snit)   & the anniversary of the last time it was
forgotten or not   on purpose or not

take your time   & guess what today is   dunno   that s why you
guess   & while you re at it try guessing the time

on the way to my pickup   i am confronted & confused by the old guy
(at least as old as i)   in the parking lot   who asks me for the
timeoday & then says   (!) damn   that reminds me that i may
have almost outlived my relevance   i thought i still had time
cause i have been on good terms with   good ol' mountain-standard
[but   (?)whom can you trust to trust you these days]

still   in puertorico they don t do daylight savings   so
look for me there   where my freshness date won t have expired

3.18.21

(!)not

another change of seasons ɔoem   i quit that many seasons ago
but i m renewing my vow   i won t do it   i m accused enough
of repeating myself [myself]   (!)fine   got the message   i ll clamp
my yap   i order myself   NO season cusp sappiness   NO similes
of anticipation or regret   comings & goings   migratory departures
& arrivals   talk about repetition   (!)holy shit   i m up to here ←
with it   (!) but   oh   am I glad that like reluctant lovers
won by patience not by coaxing the seasons change

5.12.21

i know

i know   i should stop complaining   & i don t want to sound negative
about trying to be upbeat so i ll maintain a jolly demeanor as i refuse
to be gloriously happy   when i stub my toe on a metaphorical stone
but remember i was awarded this life accidentally & then against my
will it became my responsibility   & worst of all i must continue to
try to correct its course before the final blunder

4.10.21

(?) have we met

there s something about yo_   as if we have shared our thoughts
as if we had argued   then agreed   as if you had granted me
leave to borrow your paper & pen   & to consult your muse &
voice   i appreciate your generosity   & in turn will honor your
wishes to keep secret your hidden promises   & not disturb your
quiet afternoons   by promcting my own preferences   good then
& thank you for the nod of familiarity

4.7.21

(!)oh this bright day

from the hilltop i can see farther than speculation
to where i am lost in the cuts &   gullies &   gaps
&   washes &   the filigreed mystery of
sublimating snow   in the wind shadow   past
sagebrush   a cursive scrollwork of cryptic
(symbols)
                        & yes   i have not forgotten
                              another spring blizzard
                            gathers to the southeast
                        & you surely know   i know
the shimmer of this warmth   will be chased from
the basin by nightfall   while the old champ
winter still has fight in him &   as the lights dim
the hopeful fans place their bets   & yearn for
an overthrow

3.12.21

mulligrubs

midafternoon   accuse the
day s passage   admit failures
imminent   &   endless
    appeal the   sunset
to   hurry   avoid promises
        avow   indifference
        assign   tomorrow
        its own   devices

6.29.20

express briefly

that color   it s in the east   that color   just after the sun dips below
the western peaks   at that particular time of evening   crepuscular
some poet might call it
                        but   that word would **overwhelm** the whole
effort   so just call that color kinda ˜ purpleish   & blueish   &
that high cloud   (some meteorologist might call it cumulus)
but that word could   **overwhelm**   the whole description   because
any person   who accidentally comes upon my attempted description
has his own   (particular cloud)   high enough   to still catch the last
light of the missing sun   that shadow is not purple & blue   it is
inside a flask of that hue looking out   & see(!) that flannel of a tree-
ripe peach on that cloud (?)   just high enough (well ˜ almost) to
catch the last light of our star   which has departed from my view
(also   it s spring & the peaches are still rockhard & green on some
impatient tree)
                    if earth s spin would slow   just long enough for me
to find the words to describe that color   (-)   not peach   but the
stain of toxic metal cadmium orange   pale from turpentine   on a
nearly clean brush   of white bristle   or a cloudfresh towel   after an
artist s day s work   (but no artist has a fresh towel   after a day s
work   for there are smudges of darkness   & disappointments
umberous ˜ oak gall & iron inky)   & no artist would use such
terms to describe the   *unfocused color in the east*   hopeful with
loss & departing toward night
                        those words   that might **overwhelm**
the description of that   color   on the high convolution of that cloud
(already pulsing with evening lightning)   &   i won t describe
it   that description would crush the color from the pigment   &
if someone read my description   she would go to her box with the
crumpled tubes of paint to see if i limned well but would not see the
color because   its already   too late   now

5.20.20

poe s black birds

test invisible strings   above roadkill   there s no intimation
of the departed lenore   nor the cause
6.3.20

consider

m dears (and then dismiss)   t i m e expands & contains all
impatience

the subtlety which distinguishes
(")are we there yet(?") from
(")why aren t we there yet(?")

    (disappears)

one thought :   arrivals depart   departures begin to decay
immediately   until the final disappearance   which dangles
from a sky hook   reeled in on a spider s shortening cable

5.22.20

an itch

demonstrates a
perfectly coordinated world

i arrive in the
garden simultaneously with the
fly
that bites me

7.7.20

often

i ve promised brief pithy poems   still it s hard to be quick about
something (in truth) that s significant   but easy to   expatiate
about something that (truth be told) isn t   or wasn t

2.7.21

short

poems are best
nothing extraneous
this one s done
(...) almost

12.30.20

i could

go on at length about how difficult it is to write a short poem (or
for that matter any poem of any consequence at all)   & at
other times   & elsewhere   no one has been helpful   except
once   with a shout of quit bellyaching &   shut the fuck up &
then proposed self extermination   (which wasn t necessarily
metaphorical or helpful)   so i ll stop here   (or soon)   for
this bellyaching verse has grown longer than it deserves

3.28.21

instructions

for the wind are posted somewhere (if they haven t blown away) & if
i recall the pre requisites
                (")   wind must have
                a place to come from
                &   a place to go
                otherwise   no wind   (")
weather maps & prognostications are unnecessary   on this small
prominence in the prairie   we are temporarily impeding wind s
transition   that is all we need to know

5.21.20

quiet

thin   reluctant
           horizontal→
not interrupting the sun   refusing to participate in anything too
dramatic

this   after all that bluster & pushiness yesterday   when we shouted
(" ! ") enough, already   received & acknowledged   you
could have fooled me   what agency we must have   here at the
                   ←edge of the world   where no one is
watching

12.30.20

always

a worn cliché about the weather   everyone acknowledges even
encourages with a smile & a nod as if it were a codex for decryption
of some meteorological mystery swaddled in yearning
                                                   which often leads
to interpreting signs   the shape of clouds
                                        the first favorite migratory bird
                                            the first clutch of phlox
                                            the first serious intention
                                   to get the seeds started in a flat
on the sunny side of the house   or some random arthropod astir
an exposed eft shiny and blind in the afternoon brilliance
the ritual of postponing rituals
the deception that there is still plenty of time

4.27.21

the wind s

chilly corundum scrubs away bad ideas & cautions
against hopeful doubts   a mantra echoes because
the lessons have departed   though some are
still entangled in the barbed wire   whipped
& shredded while the wind   gulps another breath

11.13.20

about

that verse a couple of days ago
about some of the missing   it
wasn t about them   or about
me   it was mostly about the
echo   about the unspoken
(?)remember me

it was about   duty
it was out of   duty

5.26.20

did i

ever mention dread   the inevitable
sadness before the event(?)   as
i grew up   grew old   did
i ever mention dread (?)   inevitable is
the word for it   did
i ever mention the inevitable
angles that foreshadow
night (?)

5.28.20

sadness

my companion   constantly tainting brilliance with grey

(?)why do you undermine the footing   (?)why are you
the sluice of future s uncertain fanfare   at the precipice
roughly   joyfully   showing the edge to an interloper

11.19.20

history

instructs with shame &   steel

tem   porary measures (:)
blindness of soul   a purge
of empa   thy   ignorance
imposed   & embraced
the salve   of inventions

but   wall fissures shimmer
darkly   & seep the past s
bitter vapors   forgotten
& unforgiven

6.20.20

ice s insistence

fissures boulders   accidentally called history   water polishes
the detritus   deceit settles   ←   ∞   →   into the voids & niches
adjusting   rearranging   supporting   sustaining   [by   simple or
sinister subterfuge]

*

at that interface   retrospection insists on   the
premeditation of accidents

*

the chaos of entropy   (S)   recalls &
denies discoveries   (by degrees of depletion)

*

still   (?) why do i
think i could do better   had i another lifetime   or 2 (two)   &
the means by which i might consult anyone who had any idea

3.20.21

not just

aversion   or repugnance   or animosity   & more buried   in
unreasoning darkness where the blind expression of rage is chilled
deliberate & methodical   what misery seeps from the rotten
suppurations of our species   & what immunity do any of us attend
that cannot be breached by the infection of hate   o pity that we
were ever granted consciousness & will   however   on a
happier note...

4.9.21

(?) are you watching

humans are the
human

problem   not the
problem solvers

the trouble is   we are
the trouble   (?)is

the difference
the difference   &

not the same   &
not ourselves   (!) oh glory (!)

love defeats love   love yearns   aches

                                               unrelieved   & by relief
                                               unembraced   crushed by

parts of
premeditations while

we watch
ourselves

impotently watching

7.23.20

adjustments

after the critical moment passes   are normal
                & everything returns to normal & my outrage at my
                        own inabilities normally wouldn t last this
long- →

i have the energy for my tasks   while time slides on   spent of its
urgency   so here i am   & the only thing that s changed is that the
list of indignities is longer   & my species' mirror of shame is
(almost) as shameful as my inertia

i d consider withdrawing from membership   but my outrage will
be resurgent & strident at the next crisis   when i ll grow hoarse
in protest   (?) but then what

3.27.21

my wishes

only the ← past
present & future → &
in be(time)tween

(?)must i choose
alas   i ve been chosen

7.2.20

arrived

pretending i m the alien pre tending to be me   the sound of time s
joy is the singalongsong   no help just to be helpful   with the
exception of deception for fun

                              (?) which is better   the cure
or pre   tending to be cured

7.1.20

memory

       an image of   a reflection forgotten   &   reconstituted
recollected   as a redaction of a fiction   the hypostasis will be
or (to put it succinctly) it
was the resistance to a reaction   & the reintegration of   what
remained

7.10.20

yesterday

(hardly noticed)

as tilt shunned daylight & the horses were hayed earlier   chickens
went → to roost before the roast was Δ done   i guess saturnalia be-
gan   but out here   isolated   though still speaking
all 2 of us forgot to remind each other to join in   the celebration

12.18.20

new year

(?) really
as if the old one was   used   beyond further
                    use   for
   economy s sake we   used   to wear hand- me-
                                    ↓downs
            making   use   of something well broken in
patched on the elbows   buttons replaced unmatched
                 no   use   complaining
          we were   used   to it & we lived with what we got
just as we will with a   new year

1.1.21

marks

on the year s arc don t demand observations   much less insights

at the last winter solstice i was beset merely by indifference   but a
year has passed   &   right now is the anniversary of what i didn t
know then   when i was n t here yet   &   the plague wasn t there
yet   so   from that perspective   the plague is here   & now i m
almost wherever else i might be   on this shortest day of the year
which is exactly where i was last year at about this time
                                                                                memory is a
filter of large & irregular perforations   entangling some things
while others escape   don t ask me what i remember of the past
year   ask me what i ve forgotten

12.21.20

day end

at the spring   cold   slipping into the draw   horses drink through
a hole in the ice
                              which reminds me   that my mate
reminds me to hydrate   it s one of her campaigns

12.30.19

(?)what is

more horizontal than the prairie
(?)what is more vertical than a thunderhead
(?)what is more diagonal than pythagoras
(?)is anything more infinite than an asymptote
(?)or wetter than a great thirst
slaked

7.10.20

the mind

of a suicide s   not always
decipherable   though   a gun fallen from the
hand   or an   empty pill bottle by the sofa   or
chin up   suspended   tiptoe   or
vitality   seeping   away from a vein (or 2)
open   in a scarlet   hottub   stereo playing   the
intention s pretty clear   but

the local paper said the
man on the motorcycle
not   wearing a helmet   swerved
across   the center line   into an
oncoming pickup truck   a
midafternoon accident   on
                                    a clear day

7.10.20

dialectics

my darlings   we are the persistence of
the   departing presence   the
uncancelled silence   we

                        get old & arrive
at crazy

           (?)which one cures the other

resisting   arriving before
leaving   nodding   stirring
deferring

7.19.20

edits

& rewrites are deceptive   if i believe i m making improvements
it s more accurate to say   i m being punished for having nothing to
say   (but i should attempt to say it as well as i can)
            for if by chance   by not saying nothing   i miss
                        saying something worth
                        saying i ll
regret it ever after   but at my age   not for long   *ex nihilo*

2.16.21

welcome

to an old friend whose voice rises from the sump & says (" ")   i
told you so   & comforts by asking   (" ? ")   what did you expect
maybe &   (" ? ")   what was the question   & don t waste my time
& don t fool yourself   so   i ll commiserate briefly because it s clear
that neither of us ever speaks to clarity
                                        that s out of the question

(?) what would be the point anyway   just between the two of us   but
be brief   duty echoes   i m going

12.27.20

sometimes

it s surprising how it comes in small installments   first an
errant bump   around which time curls   eddies   &   sinks
then the cracks &
voids   impediments in the interstices   details & repetitions   the
[illusion] incomplete   but still ineluctable   &   as bright as night
with the question   (?) what s so surprising

1.16.21

trimming

the margins of a photograph   (?)what is removed   taken away
(?)who weeps beyond excision s edge   while
                                centered
is focused a smile   (?)unseen   who yawns with indifference
at the enacted art & levity of the featured subject   (?)who
reminds him of who he was   while he denies who he is

2.2.21

contact

with my past life by contacting past contacts   (?)do i
support their version of me by reviving my version of them   &
(?)in order to remind me that it is i who they remember will they
remind me of myself as i remember them knowing me

2.3.21

the point

i get it   nothing to say   & expansively said with little to avow
on
  a
   footworn path   profligacy posing as promise

8.6.20

a buff chicken

in the sun on a
chill morn standing on one
leg   the toe of the other foot
extended   touching the
frozen ground for
                    balance
is a
lesson

equilibrium might
come naturally
if not sought with
too much
purpose

9.9.20

old dog

comes out→ with me to do chores in the evening
still a dog   first she   sniffs
                                         nosing the breeze
stands unsteadily   & a little humpedup   she
shivers   can t hear my voice when i say
(were done)   let s go back in ←

                           the nasturtium sky
                                    slips
                           ~~behind the hill~~   ▲
she s ready for a nap

old dog has the courage to face failure   on
another outing   she might have the energy
to teach me   a new trick

2.26.21

spring snow

different   almost friendly   but not a friend   (?)what re
the criteria for friendship   not impatient   mostly predictable
reassuringly good natured   a little foolish   carelessly fearless

old dog   confounded   left another   pile of shit on the floor
(?)would a friend do that   this one   (confused in her
departing vitality) did   i cursed   (?)did i say
(friends have a way of testing your patience)   i aimed her
toward the door & out   then i cleaned up the mess

she always barked to be let in so   i waited   finally   i
went to the door to call her   outside   facing away from the
porchlight   she stared   with nearly sightless eyes into the
night   her back damp with wet spring snow

                                        i guided her in
dried her off   then to her bed   she sat   waited
finally   her front legs folded   she found a
position   i patted her gently   to let her know i was there
it mattered to me   that i believed it   mattered to her

i tried to sleep in a chair close by   while   her breath
came   in small gasps   through most of the night
then intermittent   & after 3   finally ceased

old dog   with a last trick for a friend   a perfect departure
into her own darkness   on the first attempt

3.16.21

69

ah death

you re everywhere   ← ↑ ↓ →   good of you to be respectful of
silence   those who hear a clanging buzz in their ears as you enter
must admit too late that it s the mute noise of inevitability

yes   always on call   never a respite   you bear your responsibilities
in good spirits & without complaint   a champion   smiling through
adversity   you re there   for those who hope   maybe even
believe   that they have been left behind   or forgotten

5.1.21

=equations

e g
i feed the hens while
three rose finches wait on the
snowy rail of the
chicken yard

a
fourth finch
arrives

they readjust

w a i t i n g
is now longer by $\frac{1}{4}$
of a wait

12.11.20

y see

      i was headed down the hill to feed the hens   & there were 5 antelope over the fence   in the next pasture   standing in the sagebrush watching me   so i stopped halfway down the hill to watch them   & it occurred to me that they knew i was watching them watch me   so i continued watching them watch me watching them for a little while

& then they ran a short distance   & stopped & another antelope joined them   so now i saw that there were actually   6 antelope watching me   watch them

4.18.21

tendrils

blind curls   bind the
wire

(?) spirals of habit
strong (or not) enough to
hold by hopeful deceits &
                desperate
                helicals
the
globed squash
growing suspended
on the garden wire

8.12.20

i dreamed i

looked at the speedometer numbers & chided my father not to
drive so fast   he never did   he was pokey on the road
slow in his old age   no drama from a good and honest man &
no fatal crash

he died in bed   in 1990   dreaming   i hope

9.20.20

i dreamed

it was my turn to go   but i couldn t hold my breath long
enough   then   i remembered the revolver which my
friend had used for his departure   all the chambers
(but one) were   empty & it had a spent casing   i woke
from the apnea   grateful that no one had
                                        witnessed my cowardice
i promised to practice my suicide   think it through   so
i d be better at it

next time.

8.22.20

stanza

a unit   or sub unit reprised for
repetition
tier
on
tier
forming a more
elaboratestructuralevent   that
by its imposing size & recapitulation
it s height & width & habit   seems
permanent or at least   purposeful &

casts a long shadow   where nothing
grows & in whose shelter a snarling
beast paces   jowls wetslick   &
fanged

8.31.20

morning silence

(tinnitus louder than the
birds outside)   pretending
stealth   practicing the
refraction of focus

at the colloquium of
my thoughts   not a participant   only
an observer with a
plastic *visitor* s i d
on my pocket s hem

the participants are courteous
we re all   listening   not
interrupting

9.17.20

without

words stewed in the bile of disgust   sublimated into pitiful protest
the kin of my species seek gainful employment as death camp guards
& purveyors of small bandages & large excuses
                                        (?)am i   even a
whining voice pleading to the convinced & unconvicted

11.3.20

regret

the burden for tomorrow
                    carried from this present pause
                                        in layers of
accumulating detritus
                    hope s buoyant balloons
                                        perforated by reality

opportunities are not serendipitous anchors
                                in the sludge
                                                merely
smaller accidents
                sucked into the vortex of the larger mistake

                                                        o sun
fairest of witnesses
                    noticing all
                                silently regarding everything
rewarding nothing

11.6.20

don t

tell anyone not to tell anyone that we could be wrong   been that
before without admitting it & no credit for naming it   dead end
we re nearly there   almost

9.3.20

things

shrink   turn dark   sag   desiccate   the

first chilly morning of autumn   reminds
me   of that day   from which i won t
report back   though i won t be
very busy

9.7.20

after

the premature killing freeze my garden s
inspiration for   pointless philosophical
utterances   choking paroxysms of
metaphors offering insight into something
(... anything at all) in the   ▥   rectangle
of my tillage   seems to have run it s course
of course   i ll wait   but   expect   (nothing)

9.10.20

(?)only

    2 days → to go until the day after tomorrow
when the observation will be made that tomorrow
was allowed to linger for an extra day before
       it was swept into the trash along with
the (!)promise to try to do better

9.20.20

starting

½ way through the question is a bad idea   but
also a good one   so confusion lingers &

(?) who s being interrogated   is partly the
answer & partly the question & what s missing
in the middle   is no puzzle   only just mostly
the lazy constituents   of a spent inquiry

so we sit across from one another   waiting
for the other to offer a suggestion

9.21.20

6 forty five &

the habit of
the shadow of the
house runs down the
hill toward the
fence   the
hens go to roost   the
horses to the
spring   persistence is a
comforting paradigm

9.21.20

O (is for) october

a smile & a wink from a former lover who
invites you for a last dalliance   then

says   (!)get lost   pal   & puts you out in

the cold

the sun disappears earlier   &   frost   if
not present again   will be presently

10.7.20

frost

dressed as a clown   a messenger in pied reflections   (?)how
do i adjust for the shadowed descent

                                    afternoon sun   flimflammer
hiding the flaws   a practiced   insincere apology   a crust of
imperfect patina
              next
                    wait for ridiculous references   & matters more
significant   (stop me if you ve heard this one)

the gaping trough intimates a chill of equinox

                                    half shuttered   eyes
smiling anticipation while

                    i trust you to watch me convince myself that
you believe that you will never leave me (again)   until the next time

10.13.20

night wind

deceives slyly   a
whistling waif sits
around the corner in
the dark   an exhaling hiss   a
slight gasp   (not alarm)

prowling dark is
only mostly silent   it
lifts↑
susurrant breath   hardly
disturbing
sleep s covers

9.30.20

(2)darkness

is the best place to wait   eyes open for [numb]   mumbled concerns
in the morning   gone   (!)ha   tricked you again(!)   deep in the
corners   < >   of shelves   in inky lacunae   hide props in the
melodrama   houselights   please   i ll find my way
out   past the masked translators   traducers   &   typecast
troublemakers

2.24.21

time s recriminations

fiddling   wasted   used up   or running out (m dash)   only
when it s too late to refuse   a twist on   the fabric s bias
bartleby incinerating (dead letters)   delayed

at the gallows   counting the seconds   dying of its own
accord   i m in no hurry but   had i the time i d attempt
further explanations

9.28.20

idling

the preferred way to do nothing   it s product is weightless
requires no pretending   is quickly forgotten

                                        significance should not
encumber
idleness   loading an empty container with slop & sediment
makes it burdensome & boring   regrettably ready to obscure
the idle moment s meaning   by imposing meaning s weight

9.25.20

trapezoid

is the best geometry   a truncated pyramid   missing an apex
aspirations   abandoned incom (plete)   a full effort shirked
a good rationalization wasted in reflection   a halfhearted
attempt

trapezoidal s   the shape on the floor   of the sun through→ the
kitchen window   lengthening as it departs

trapezoidal s the shape of a righteous quarrel   that is not
triangulated & looses its impetus   before it gains a conclusion
then   goes with a shrug to the   oh never mind   file

10.11.20

past noon

routine & gerontological   pandered or pitied a shift from plans &
perspectives   just finish one project   events episodic not
programmatic   (a vignette before naptime)   (an installment)

with resignation & boredom   by droning phone call   a cousin
has died   & his wife is relieved   reciting his long misery
detail by detail   (& finally freed from & so on and so forth...)
pitied & pandered (a vignette before naptime)

the casuistry of the cousin s
response   (well, still upright and taking nourishment) the last time
we spoke   (how we lie to each other)

i slowly realize   that suddenly i m growing older   again

10.20.20

they re doing

it   friends & acquaintances are dying   this is what happens
        live &   add to death s chances   there are pauses
(no hurry)   but it ll get us   saw it   in the newspaper
a conversation   a phone call   [(?) oh did you hear]
                                                        my place in
the rank s unknown   (?) will i see it coming   & when i find out
won t i be too preoccupied decaying   that i won t share the news

            (?)whose friend or acquaintance am i   that someone
might regret (or not) hearing of it   or more likely ponder my name
with a question inflection

1.25.21

that

was yesterday   so quiz me when we get there   otherwise
i fear you ll convict me of blamelessness while i m dreaming

5.23.21

messages

during this isolation fit the lifestyle   i m
                    surprised
by any call on my cellphone that   isn t   robotic and mercantile
      email: somehow i m on some send-all lists   the
camaraderie of myriad cadres of recipients   [hi out there
i was just thinking of you among the thousands   dead and alive that
my random email might have reached]   [as i sat with morning]
coffee   looking out the back window   your signal was interrupted
by a message from an eagle   which descended to scavenge the
corpse of a deer on the far side → of the hill
                              message received & acknowledged
eagle departs with a crawfull   noon approaches cautiously
(check spelling   then send)

2.26.21

this is

a message   (in case the plague should take me)   an
(envelope) on my cluttered desk   just some final details

— that s danny s phone #   tell him where to send the backhoe
— if by predilection   or for pleasure   or just habit   you wish
    to insist on the obverse of anything i ve said   feel free
—oh & i love you   but i ve said enough   still   i
    almost forgot   after sundown don t ~~FORGET~~ to [close]
    the henhouse against ← ↙ ↑ → predators   after all   someone
    will need (not to forget   to remember to)   do it

1.9.21

fortunate for all

that quite a while ago i gave up trying to memorialize or interpret
the little cyphers of bird footprints in the snow   but in those
days i never met a metaphor i didn t like   & believed i needed a
relationship with nature   to try to revivify my poetic sense of
the world

that confusion abided until i found   that the hidden meanings
of sunsets   prairie sparrows & the like   do very well without
my assistance   now
              i sleep soundly   reassured that the bird
tracks   like little tritons   will be there [bright&early] in the
A M fully significant of their own significance   without
the encouragement of a single simile

3.10.21

on valentine s day

i stand in the snow
& it s subzero & windy
& i m wearing a union suit under my jeans
& i m shivering   for no particular reason i think of
shackleton s stranded men   brave beyond madness   but without
the insulation of double kn t   or a hot shower waiting   after
failing to negotiate the gaps in their clothing   & pissing on
themselves   down there   south   of the antarctic

                    cir le
in 1916   for them this day would have been late summer
& i m still a union man   solidarity forever with matters of faulty
judgement   & when call d upon   may i be that brave

2.14.21

it s nice

how on average   things seem to turn out
heatwave/coldsnap   comes to moderation
gale versus silent stillness   just enjoying the breeze
bluesky to the edge   after a
three day   blindingblizzard   gets ya partly cloudy & a rising
barometer

a leap forward   then sliding

← backward   but we re
holding our own   barely
brilliant & insightful confronts
dull & pedestrian   middling to mediocre   strike up
the bland

(?) is it too early   to leave   i don't want to be late

7.31.21

despite

the present efforts of resistance   disappointments arrive daily X
X X X

inured   but instructed by their persistence   if a day arrives when
they re absent   their absence won t disappoint me

3.12.21

1 the county

               road & bridge department sent its experts   & its
graders   smoothing down the corrugations on the gravel road i
travel   when i leave my prairie home

2 not because i ve been complaining   still   they reduce the rippling
washboard & are governed   by a schedule   the county roads
are on rotation   & complaints are not uncommon

3 experience informs their cycle   vehicles shimmy sliding
no control accelerating   drivers struggle steering badly   losing
traction if they re speeding

4 unexpected outcomes follow   dental fittings leaving molars
lenses vibrating in glasses   & carefully capped coffee containers
lose their contents without warning

5 but   there s still that old conundrum   if *here* were nt *here*
& *there* not *there*   then no need to try to join them   the county
road & bridge department   could better use it s time attempting

6 plans for absent final outcomes   or for posting signs at sundown
helping pilgrims as they wander   seeking meanings for existence
missions without explanation

7 but   instead the experts came from the road & bridge
department   blades on graders angled sharply   came smoothing
out peaks & valleys of the road i sometimes travel

8 so   then when i need to leave from *here* & eventually get to
there   to do the things that i must do   or possibly retrace
my route   in case there s something i ve left out

5.9.21

in the

night   lines composed challenge the morning s memory   &
what seemed brilliant in the dark   is merely absence s
smoldering wick   with effort its replacement is roused &
shortly judged lacking   thus verses of significance &
sensibility remain sequestered   secret   unsung   their
attendant fame still missing

                            a friend encourages   a journal &
pen at   bedside
                  i say nc   more satisfying to have claimed
a genius effort   than to have written proof it was otherwise

7.6.21

regarding reality

(?) who makes such claims   (?) who has the credentials   (?) who
has published the standards against which i may judge the day to day
silence confronting my questions   which leaves me no choice but to
make protest   informal but affirmative   fronting the mirrored
interlocutor & not taking no/or yes for an answer   be warned   i
am impatient   no/or yes is unacceptable   alternatives to no/or yes
must surely exist in the drawer of alternatives   &   there must be
other possibilities too   far too many   to outline in this brief...

4.7.21

progress

is possible   (if i m not mistaken)   & i can learn from my mistakes
i ll make an effort to make this verse better than the last one   so
this current one   though less than poetic won t be belabored
because less effort expended means an economy of means   &
should i decide to persist   failing to succeed   nearly effortlessly
is not out of the question

4.12.21

the urge

to poetry should evoke caution s claxon   just as a deceptively
attractive moment may be the portal to perdition   the results of
veering accidentally into the pathway of the muse   are almost
always better stockpiled   like survival supplies against the future
hoping never to be needed
                                however   not unlike a bibulous reformer
who finds an excuse to stray   or a dieter who yearns for that
certain missing delicious something   a poet s urges
are hard to suppress   all the more reason to seek desperate
handholds on craggy stones   or to grasp for slippery roots   while
rotating in the vortex of the dark eddy
                                & finally   resignation

like one condemned   whose penultimate gasp pleads innocence
but whose final groan asks   ? after all   what s the worst
that can happen   9.14.21

www.ingramcontent.com/pod-product-compliance
Lightning Source LLC
Chambersburg PA
CBHW030756150426
42813CB00068B/3181/J